Code Samples

The New Professional Programmer's Guide

Ellen Guon Beeman

Code Samples

Editor: JoanneMachin.com
Cover art: Phoenix McCollough
Formatting: Nina Pierce of Seaside Publications
ninapierce.com/book-formatting/

ISBN 9798619601442

First Edition
Washington, USA

Code Samples

This short book is about code samples and how they can help you get the programming job you want. Code samples are a potentially useful tool for a job-seeking programmer at any stage of their career, but especially for the computer science student who is graduating college.

In this book, you'll see how to identify and craft the best possible code sample, see examples of code samples in C++ and C#, and learn from interviews with technical managers who hire programmers and software engineers who have successfully navigated the hiring process using their code samples.

This book is available for free to the students and alumni of DigiPen Institute of Technology. If you are a "DigiPen Dragon" and are unable to get an electronic or print copy from our college library, please contact me directly.

www.EllenBeeman.com

Contents

Dedication

This book is dedicated to my sisters, Laura Guon Bondarevsky and Micki Zaritsky,

and my friends, Jen Klier, Bryce Maryott, S.R. "Randi" Randall, Cal Reinhard, Rachel Rutherford, Lisa "Cloud" Smith, and Melissa Mead Tyler,

with deepest thanks for your support during difficult times.

Acknowledgments

Many thanks to my friends and colleagues who contributed to this book: Nate Cleveland, Rick Lambright, Amelia Laumann, Christopher Onorati, Cal Reinhard, Justin Riccardo, and Judy Tyrer. And many thanks to my advance readers Eric Fleegal and Bryce Maryott, editor Joanne Machin, layout designer Nina Pierce, and cover designer Phoenix McCollough.

Special thanks to all of the students, faculty, staff, and alumni of DigiPen Institute of Technology. You inspire me every single day.

PART ONE

All About Code Samples

Introduction

This short book is about code samples and how they can help you get the programming job you want.

The inspiration from this book came from an unlikely source. My friend Cal Reinhard and I had just finished our talk and demo on whiteboard programming interviews at the 2018 Game Developers Conference. That's our big national annual conference for the video games industry, filled with sessions about technical and creative topics, and I've been fortunate to be a speaker at this event many times.

After our talk, a college student came up to me and asked me how he should approach his job hunt. What should he prepare in addition to his resume? What would increase his likelihood of getting an interview for a programming job? How could he stand out from all of the other junior programmer candidates when he's applying for the job he really wants?

My answer was immediate. I didn't even have to think about it before I said: "Write some good code samples."

Everyone knows you need a resume (or CV) to get an interview. But you shouldn't stop with that. You should have a "programmer portfolio" website where you demonstrate the many reasons why an employer should interview you. Code samples are a great addition to a job-hunter's website. A good code sample won't necessarily get you the job, but it can help you get the interview.

Your best interview scenario is when the employer already knows they want to hire you before they've even met you. You have the skills they need, and they're hopeful that you'll be a good fit for their software team. They're just confirming that you would be a great hire by meeting you in person.

But software companies are also absolutely terrified of hiring a programmer who isn't merely incompetent, but actively detrimental to the project and team. Because that really does happen.

I've worked with dozens of amazing programmers on various projects throughout my video games career, along with a few astonishingly bad ones. My nickname for this type of person was "The Nightmare Programmer Hire." I have, regretfully, worked with more than one of these, but I'll describe one of the worst. This particular programmer was on our project for a full year. After several months of working together, I started to raise some concerns about this person's code. I was seeing some odd code behaviors, some strange bugs, unhandled edge cases, and some other things that made me a little twitchy. One of the senior programmers did an in-depth code review, and soon after, they decided to fire this programmer and rip out all of the code. All of it! A year's worth of work by this individual. The icing on top of this very unpleasant cake was that this same senior programmer rewrote the person's entire system from scratch, in only about one month.

If you want to demonstrate that you are definitely NOT that "Nightmare Programmer Hire," a code sample is one way to show that you can do the work for a prospective employer. But it's more than that. A code sample is an opportunity to show who you are and what skills you bring. It's a way to help convince an employer that they should hire you even before they actually meet you.

Why Code Samples?

Code samples are potentially useful for a job-seeking programmer at any stage of their career, including:

- **Students who are applying for internships or will be graduating from college soon.** These are the people I work with the most frequently at the college where I teach! For students, code samples are a way to differentiate yourself from the many other applicants who are only submitting a resume listing the college courses they've completed, and nothing else.

- **Veteran coders who need to demo work that isn't restricted under an employer's Non-Disclosure Agreement (NDA).** If all your recent work is required to stay confidential, you may want something to show where there's no question that you have the legal right to show it to a prospective employer. Never do anything that violates an NDA or take code samples from a previous employer without written approval. (Basically, don't do anything that would qualify you for my rather infamous annual "How to Get Fired" lecture at my college!)

- **Veteran coders who want to demonstrate a specific coding skill to a prospective employer.** You may want to show your skills in a particular programming language. You may want to show that you can handle a specific type of coding problem if you don't already have professional experience working on that kind of project.

What Are Your Goals?

Before you even create your first code sample, there are some questions you can start thinking about:

- What kind of programming job are you looking for?

- Have you researched the companies you'll be applying to?

- What programming languages do they use?

- What kind of code samples would help you get that job?
- Should you create or tailor a code sample for that specific company?

The Basics of Code Samples

My recommendation for a good code sample, which I have described many times to my students at DigiPen Institute of Technology:

"Solve one specific problem with code that is clean, concise, and well-commented."

That's it! Shouldn't be hard, right? Now we'll discuss each part of that in more detail.

"Solve One Specific Problem..."

You want to find an interesting problem to solve. As much as I'm fond of the famous "FizzBuzz" problem, and often use it for practice sessions when one of my students is first learning how to do the whiteboard programming interview, it's not what you want for a code sample. ("FizzBuzz" will make its appearance at the very end of this book, and also in my next book, which will be on technical interviewing!)

"Interesting and unusual" is likely a good way to go. My favorite example is also the one that convinced me of the value of code samples many years ago. Nate Cleveland is a wonderful former colleague of mine. He applied to Monolith/Warner Bros and submitted his code sample of an "A* pathfinding algorithm implementation written in Python" with his application. It was several pages of smart, clean, and perfectly commented code, and it definitely helped him get his interview. You'll hear more about Nate and this particular code sample later in this book.

"... *With Code That Is Clean...*"

"Clean code" means code that is well-organized, uses standard nomenclature, and is broken intelligently into clear segments that each handle a specific task. The logical structure is important. Don't worry about the code being really sophisticated. What you want is clarity, readability, and internal consistency. Everything should appear to have been written from a single style guide.

"... *Code That is Concise...*"

Concise means short! Seriously, your code sample should be several hundred lines of code at most. We'll talk about sharing full GitHub code bases for entire projects later in the book, but to start, I recommend creating a short code sample.

Concise also means structurally tight. *Never* do any "copy and paste" code in your code sample. A terrible example of this would be handling keyboard input by duplicating a line of code for each individual key on the keyboard. Make sure you're handling everything in a smart, efficient way.

"*... And Code That is Well-Commented*"

This could easily be the biggest challenge and one that may be the hardest for you. Let's be realistic here. You're probably going to write code that you don't comment as well as you should at some point in your life, but to quote Aragorn from one of my beloved *Lord of the Rings* movies: "It is not this day!"

Seriously, you <u>need</u> to comment the $#%@ out of your code sample.

Companies know that sometimes you're going to be rushed when you're writing code, or have to implement a quick fix. You will also write code that is "obvious" when someone reads it in the context of a greater project. When that happens, you won't necessarily comment your code all that well. However, no one wants to hire someone that they KNOW won't comment their code, especially if they see that in a code sample.

When you are commenting code, at a minimum, you should write comments that explain each function. For a code sample, I recommend much more extensive commenting.

Your first comment should be an introduction and description of the code sample and what problem or need you're trying to solve with it. Insert another short description for each block of code. Write lines of comments throughout the code for anything that could use clarification.

You should answer these questions in your introduction:

- What is a brief description of this code sample?
- What are you trying to accomplish?
- What is the clever part of this code sample, and what are you the most proud of?
- What did you learn while writing this code?

That last item can be tremendously important: what did you learn while creating this code sample? As I've already mentioned, the code sample does more than just show that you can code; it can demonstrate your personality and why you would be a good hire. This is from the introduction to the unit test code sample written by my former student Justin Riccardo: "This was my first time learning about how unit tests work and how to integrate Google Test into a project. I enjoyed making unit tests and discovered that I enjoy SDET (test automation programming) work."

What is Justin demonstrating here with that description of his code sample? Enthusiasm, eagerness to learn, willingness to test his own code, and that he enjoys writing test tools! This short excerpt provides a wonderful amount of information for a prospective employer. With just those few sentences, Justin demonstrated many of the traits of a terrific junior programmer hire.

Comments matter. Think of your code sample, and especially how you document it, as all being part of the actual job interview. It's an interview where you aren't present, but the employer is making decisions about whether to interview and hire you.

And Write Good Comments!

Always make sure your comments make sense, and aren't in-jokes or obscure references. You may think you're writing comments for some future colleague who is going to have to update your code, but really, you're writing it for yourself, your future self, that person who will say, "I'm frustrated trying to figure this code out and it's 3 a.m. and I'm really tired!"

Don't put jokes in your comments. I'm going to admit one of the most embarrassing things I ever did in my entire career—I am still very embarrassed by this all these years later. I repeatedly wrote the comment "Do not remove this on pain of Tickle-Death" into the *Wing Commander II* code base. Admittedly, if you did anything to that part of the code, the game would fail to compile, so Tickle-Death could be considered appropriate. (Well, maybe? Honestly, no! I'm just trying to justify what I did.)

That code was used in derivative projects and ported to half a dozen different hardware platforms by various teams. A lot of people saw those goofy and incomprehensible comments of mine. Over the years many people have contacted me to ask what the @#$& I meant by those bad code comments.

So... don't do what I did on the *Wing Commander II*. There I was, working with this amazing team on a fantastic award-winning game that has been rated one of the top 100 games of all time... and I was writing really stupid and useless comments into the code base!

About Commenting Ratios

The next question is, "Are you commenting enough?" It's easy enough to run an app like CLOC (Count Lines of Code) on your code sample, and see what your ratios are between code and comments. Ratios are tricky to use as a rule of thumb—there will be code that needs less commenting, and code where you want to heavily comment it, possibly even more than the total lines of code itself.

For my students I generally recommend a ratio of at least 4 to 1 between lines of code and comments, as in, for every four lines of code, write a comment. It's a very rough approach, but it can be a good starting guideline. And seriously, if you're writing at a "10 to 1" or "20 to 1" ratio of code to comments, please stop and think about whether you can do better than that! Highly descriptive variable names will only get you so far; you still need to write comments.

I'll quote my friend Bryce Maryott on this: "At the end of the day, when you've hit Save and Compile and submitted it to source control, the important thing isn't the quantity but the usefulness of the comments."

And to paraphrase Captain Barbossa from the movie *Pirates of the Caribbean*: the number of comments are "more what you'd call guidelines than actual rules."

Does It Compile?

So, here's the reality about code samples and compiling: most prospective employers won't try to compile your code. But some might. Decide upfront whether you're going to label this a "code snippet," and make it clear that it's not a complete program and it won't compile, or plan for it to be compiled by one of your interviewers.

Regardless of whether your code sample can compile, it does need to be clean and have no obvious compiler errors. Overall, I recommend writing your code to compile. If nothing else, compiling your code will catch warnings and errors and allow you to fix them so your code sample will be cleaner and easier to read. Using code that actually runs correctly has the added benefit of showing genuinely functional code.

If You Don't Know What Would Make a Good Code Sample, Where Do You Start?

Here's one approach, the advice that I give to my programmer students: Just look for possible code sample topics as you're working on your regular projects. For every software project you work on, just start thinking about what part of the code might make a great code sample. If you find something that might work, then set it aside. You don't need to do anything with it yet. Just save it for later.

Your code sample can be a clever method you just came up with, or a very clean implementation of a known problem, or a type of software tool that you're really passionate about. This could be from a team project, a personal project, or something that you wrote specifically to be used as a code sample.

There are also websites with programming or math problems that could make for a good code sample. As of this writing, Project Euler (https://projecteuler.net/) is a terrific site for this.

The Brass Ring, Or Writing a Code Sample for Someone Who Isn't a Programmer

You probably just read that last line and are thinking, "What, is Ellen crazy?" Well, yes. But I'm also recommending that you write your code sample so someone who is not a programmer can read and understand it.

Why? Because the very first person who is likely to see your resume and code sample at a prospective employer may not be a programmer. Odds are good that this person will be a recruiter or some other non-technical person. This may be someone who works for the company's Human Resources department or is under contract to help the company find new candidates. Their job is to forward promising candidates to the hiring manager, the person who is managing the process of hiring new programmer candidates. That "hiring manager" might be a project manager/producer like myself, or a Lead Engineer, or Director of Technology.

But that first person who reads your code sample may think that Python is a snake and LUA is a Hawaiian barbecue party. Okay, yes, I'm exaggerating. But seriously, there is a good chance the first reader of your code sample will not be a programmer, yet this person's enthusiasm matters! They likely can't hire you directly, but they can put your resume and code samples on the top of the stack of candidates and convince the hiring manager to look at your application first. That's potentially very valuable to you.

So how do you write a code sample for a non-technical reviewer? Use human-readable variable and function names, write lots of explanatory comments, and otherwise just follow good software engineering best practices.

On the Subject of Best Practices and Supporting Materials...

The code sample is also a terrific way of demonstrating your software engineering best practices. This could be use of a software documentation tool like Doxygen, or describing how you did a code review with friends or colleagues on your code sample, or the research you did that went into writing this sample. All of that should be described in detail and considered part of your code sample.

Amelia Laumann, Technical Director at the online game company ArenaNet, said her concern with code samples is if they don't reflect that the programmer has tried to understand the problem. Amelia is also alarmed if the code only has the core component, without anything else you would expect to see created for a real project. "I get worried if I see none of the surrounding context... I want to see supporting data structures, test cases, documentation."

I strongly recommend following Amelia's recommendation to provide as much documentation and test cases for your code sample as you can. For simpler topics, this might not be needed, but for a more complex code sample, it can definitely help make the case that you're someone that this company should interview.

Let's Talk About Standards

Coding standards are practically a cause of religious war. As one former student of mine likes to say, "Of course you will use Allman braces, as [DigiPen's] Professor Mead and G-d intended!" Location of curly braces, tabs versus spaces... the arguments are endless. But I only have two opinions on coding standards in code samples:

First, and above all else, be consistent—whatever style you use, keep using that throughout the code sample.

Second, the correct answer in a programmer interview is... "Of course I will use whatever coding standards you have at your company!" Seriously, when you join a professional programming team, you need to go with the standards and conventions they've already adopted.

Now Ask For Help!

So you have a first pass at a code sample; it's written and compiles cleanly, and you've taken the time to make sure that it is beautifully commented. Now what?

Now is when you really start asking for help. Ask your programmer friends, your colleagues, your teachers, anyone you can find to review your code sample. Then ask for more help. Keep asking for help until you're confident that your code sample is as good as it can possibly be.

You don't want to take any chances with this. A good code sample will help you get the job interview. A bad code sample could guarantee that you don't.

So please make sure there are no typos, no misspellings, no missing semicolons or curly braces. Seriously. Fix all that stuff before your code sample goes out into the world as a representation of your best possible work.

PART
TWO

The
Hiring Managers

*In this section, I'll introduce several hiring managers
and interviewers, and their perspective on code samples
as part of a candidate's application.*

Nate Cleveland,
Principal Engineer

My interest in code samples as a way to hire great
programmers began when I was working in the early
2000s on *The Matrix Online*, a massively multiplayer
online game project at Monolith/Warner Bros.
Interactive Entertainment. The project was huge, so we
needed a big development team, too. I was one of the
team's producers, and in addition to other tasks, I
managed the hiring of over 40 people for our
development team, including programmer Nate
Cleveland.

Today, many years later, Nate Cleveland is a Principal
Engineer at King Games, the company best known for
the phenomenal hit game *Candy Crush*. He works in
Stockholm as part of their shared technology group,
writing code that benefits many of their game teams.

When I first met him, Nate was a very junior
programmer applying at Monolith/Warner Bros., looking
for his first job after studying computer science at

DigiPen Institute of Technology. Meeting Nate was also my first introduction to the college where I now teach! Working with Nate and other talented graduates is why I initially became an advisory board member for the college and, later, joined as faculty.

Nate's resume was accompanied by a code sample... a Python implementation of the A* (or "A-Star") algorithm for pathfinding. A* is a well-known algorithm for plotting efficient paths between multiple points or "nodes." Pathfinding is often needed for gameplay in video games for non-player characters.

I remember seeing that code sample and immediately taking it to Rick Lambright, our group's Director of Technology, and saying to him, "Rick, you have to look at this. This code is amazing."

Rick agreed, and I shared Nate's code sample with the other lead engineers, all of whom were impressed. We made the decision to bring Nate in for an interview. He was soon hired for the QA Engineering team, where he wrote code that helped us test that huge online game.

Even now, many years later, Nate still vividly remembers writing that Python sample code. I asked him why he included it as part of his job application. "The short answer is that Python was part of Monolith's job description," he said. "A* was an algorithm I knew, and was easy to visualize. The long answer starts with me wanting to be distinct from all my classmates. I was keenly aware that there were a lot of people that took the same classes as me."

For Nate, it was all about that differentiation from other students from his college and nearby colleges. "Learning skills to make myself distinct from my classmates was looming in my mind in that last year of school. An extra programming language was one of those skills, and I picked Python, based on an article by Bruce Dawson."

Nate then focused on creating code samples for prospective employers. "I wrote programs that used various popular C++ libraries of the time, and implemented algorithms in C++, A* being one of them. All of this, I did in the year before I even started looking for jobs in earnest, while I was still taking classes at DigiPen. When it came time to submit a code sample for that job at Monolith, I tried to make something specifically targeting the position from the things I knew. That was Python A*, with a very simplistic visualization."

Does Nate have recommendations for today's students, and how they might want to approach this challenge of creating code samples to help them get a programming job? "For creating code samples, I would say be mindful of any code you submit to a prospective employer," Nate explained. "I like to put all sorts of 'dumb' questions to applicants about their code sample.

Why did you make X a function, but not Y? Why did you use this container, what about that container instead? Why did you arrange the code the way you did? Why did you use this variable name here? I want to know the thought processes a developer went through, and asking every question that comes to mind is the best way I have to get that information."

Nate likes to present candidates with a coding challenge. "I also love to find bugs in an applicant's code, give them a bug report, and have them fix it for me in real time while we talk through the issue. I don't even mind that there is a small bug here and there, because mistakes happen and it's more important to see how a candidate works through a problem in a domain they are actually familiar with. I will even modify a sample or work test to have a bug, and tell them I've done so, just to create that experience."

Regretfully, Nate's "A* in Python" code sample is now lost to history, but I will always remember it and how a young programmer used a code sample to stand out from all the other candidates and secure his first professional programming job at a major game studio.

Amelia Laumann,
Technical Director

Amelia is a long-time game industry veteran who has worked for years on ArenaNet's popular massively multiplayer online game (MMO) *Guild Wars 2*. MMOs are one of the most challenging games to work on, as there are so many moving parts and different systems, ranging from billing and support systems to the actual game itself. These projects have very rigorous demands for code quality and stability. For the more successful projects, engineers will be updating and maintaining the code for many years.

When hiring a candidate, Amelia said, "Code samples are a lot of work, but they can be the difference between an average resume and [being asked to come in for] an interview." When she looks at code samples, she has a very practical way to measure what she thinks of it. "Is this code that I want to see in my code base?"

What does she like to see in a code sample? "Test cases and output that doesn't need to be compiled... because honestly, I won't compile it. A high-level description of the problem. Class projects are fine!"

Readability is extremely important. "The code should be written to be read."

One thing she says she always wants to see in a code sample: "Consistency." And she expressed concern about the ways in which a poor code sample could hurt the junior programmer job applicant. It's a red flag "if the sample doesn't reflect that the programmer has tried to understand the problem."

Amelia also recommends something that I'll talk about later in more detail: the idea of having the entire code base available publicly, not just a brief code sample. "Having a pet project on GitHub with the work history is a valuable example, without having to put in too much additional work."

In our discussion, Amelia and I also talked about one possible downside of providing code samples to an employer, which is that they may question whether you were the programmer who actually wrote the code sample. Amelia and I agree that you should be ready to discuss and elaborate upon any code samples that you present to a prospective employer as part of the interview process. So, please review your code samples before your actual interview with an employer.

Judy Tyrer,
Engineering Manager and Entrepreneur

Judy Tyrer is a long-time veteran of the game industry, having worked as a Networking Engineer at Ubisoft and then as Lead Engineer on *Magic: the Gathering: Tactics* at Sony Online. She then joined Linden Labs as Senior Engineering Manager, working on the famous *Second Life* online world. Later, she decided to found her own studio. Not being shy of challenges, her 3 Turn Productions team is working on *Ever, Jane*, a truly unique multiplayer online game based on the literary world of Jane Austen.

When it comes to hiring engineers, Judy is very straightforward about what she's looking for. "When I look at code samples, I look for best practices. Readability. And naming conventions... I don't care which you choose, as much as that you choose one." She's very clear on not including any hard-coded values, which you might need to change at a later point in the project. "No magic numbers!"

DRY (Don't Repeat Yourself) is another of her engineering philosophies. "I really, really HATE duplicate code. Blocks of 150 lines of code copy-and-pasted all over the code base with just one variable changed. If the coder doesn't understand the basic core concepts behind the code, it WILL show. I think the worst code I saw was a 64 page switch statement that I managed to get down to 30 lines of code by using this obscure little trick called... data tables."

"I prefer not to see classroom assignments. I want to see how you used code to solve a problem, to see your problem-solving skills on display," she says. "And I do like comments. 'Road not taken' comments show me that you thought it through, and didn't just bubble sort because everyone bubble sorts."

For Judy, it's all about making good decisions and explaining them in your comments. "If I see a code sample that has a comment about bench-marking results and how that made you choose a CPU-intensive solution rather than a memory-intensive one, or vice versa... you're hired!"

Rick Lambright,
Director of Technology

Rick Lambright has always been an inspiration to me, as one of the very best software engineering managers that I've ever worked with. We first worked on a team together many years ago when he was Director of Technology on *The Matrix Online*, which was my first massively multiplayer online game project, and later worked together again at Gazillion/Amazing Society on the online game *Marvel's Super Hero Squad Online*. To say that *The Matrix Online* project was an educational experience for me would be a huge understatement. I learned so much about online large-scale game technology from Rick, Toby Gladwell, Andy Kaplan, Tim Royal, David Satnik, and the many other fantastic engineers on that project. Mostly I learned that MMOs are insanely complicated, and are possibly the most technically challenging game projects you can undertake. This is why, of course, being someone who never hesitates to take on a challenge, Rick has made working on MMOs into a major part of his career.

Rick has hired dozens of programmers over the years. When looking at code samples, as with Judy Tyrer, "Don't Repeat Yourself (DRY)" also matters very much to Rick. "I'm also looking for clear flow and starting point," he said, "meaningful and consistent variable names, formatting and indentation without too-deep nesting, and code comments and documentation."

I asked Rick if he remembered Nate Cleveland's "A* in Python" code sample, which impressed me so much as a means for a very junior programmer to secure a job interview. And yes, years later, he still does. "Hah! Nate's A* was definitely memorable."

Like Nate's "A* in Python," Rick's favorite code samples are simple and use object-oriented techniques, with "bonus points for something really clever done in a very few lines of code... and commented well, of course!"

A code sample can answer hiring questions for a veteran technologist like Rick. "In general, I look for things that tell me the applicant has picked up on best practices. I realize that can be somewhat subjective, from working with professionals and/or researching coding practices on the web, such as StackOverflow.com. I always like it when they mention programmers they worked with that had good... or even bad... qualities and influences on them, and how they recognized what was good and bad."

Rick has also seen some bad code samples. "Most of the code samples I saw in my later years that I thought were truly awful came from what I would call 'old school' programmers, working mostly in more 'mature' languages like C and C++, that had been working without the daily reviews of code that you get from participating in a modern team using something like GitHub, which I've been personally using in my teams for many years."

Code reviews are tremendously valuable to Rick. "It's constantly humbling to have to defend coding practices... even if just for a silly variable name... but it has a huge influence on your final product when, like all code should be, you are forced to think about someone else maintaining it."

"One of my personal philosophies has always been to 'write code as if someone other than you will be maintaining it from day one' and 'expect whatever you write to be obsolete in 6 months or less'... in other words, don't get attached to it. While we all love programmers that 'own' their code.... frequently because nobody else wants to be messing with it... it is never, ever a good practice to let just one person maintain it. Maintenance is what a *team* does!"

But Rick has a very clear idea of what makes for the best code samples. "Something really clever... a way of solving the problem that is either new to me or that is a unique approach... even if it is less efficient but fewer lines of code. It's not essential, but it is often an indicator of someone that thinks out of the box and appreciates others who do so as well."

PART THREE

The Code Samples

In this section, I'll introduce programmers and their code samples, and the reasons why they created these for their portfolios.

Justin Riccardo,
Software Engineer

I first met Justin when he was a computer science student at DigiPen Institute of Technology. He did fantastic work on his team game projects in my classes, and when he asked for help with his job hunting, I was glad to assist him. We spent a lot of time talking about his resume, website, and especially his code samples. Since he graduated, I've had the opportunity to help him with career planning and strategies. I still remember this particular code sample that Justin wrote as a college student as one of my favorites, because it accomplishes many goals. "We were experimenting with the Google Test framework for the CS 365 Software Engineering class," he explained. "Our original assignment had us run unit tests on a small codebase. I discovered I liked making unit tests and writing test software."

Enjoying that project encouraged him to continue along the path of writing test software. "It was my first time being exposed to writing test code. I liked being able to test functions and it inspired me to apply for Software Design Engineer in Test positions when I was looking for internships and full-time work." That led directly to the creation of this test sample. "What inspired me to write that code sample was that I knew I wanted to have some piece of test code for my portfolio to show that I was interested in test software. I wanted to write a script that was simple enough for recruiters and other engineers to get an idea of what was happening in the file. So I took that binary search function from another assignment and tried to integrate it with the unit test framework."

There was a lot of learning along the way. "One thing I did learn from writing this code sample was that it was really important to name functions in a way where other developers can look at the name of it and understand what it does!"

Justin has plenty of great recommendations for young programmers. "Some advice I have for graduating students would be to make sure the code you write is well-commented. Working on bigger code repositories at my current job has taught me that it's rare to find code that is very well-commented and functions that are named appropriately. I would suggest graduating students use comments on code that is especially hard to follow, and use #define on magic numbers so that the person who has to read your code isn't confused on why a hard-coded number was used."

"Unit Test" code sample
by Justin Riccardo

```
/ * * * * * * * * *


Below is implementation for unit testing a
basic binary search. In each unit test, I am
trying to see if the basic functionality
works and testing for conditions that could
break the program. The different types of
test I used were: finding a value in and not
in the array, value at the beginning of the
array, value in an odd length array, and an
empty array. This was my first time learning
about how unit tests work and how to
integrate Google Test into a project. I
enjoyed making unit tests and discovered I
enjoy SDET work.
 * * * * * * * * * * /

#include "gtest/gtest.h"
#include "gmock/gmock.h"
//case where we didn't find the value in the
array we're looking in #define KEY_NOT_FOUND
-1
//the different types of arrays we will be
testing
int regular_array[] = {5, 10, 15, 20};
int odd_length_array[] = {1, 5, 7};
int array_with_negative_values[] = {-7, -5,
-1};
int* nullArray[5] = { NULL };
int initialized_array[5] = {};

int main(int argc, char** argv)
{
        ::testing::InitGoogleTest(&argc,
```

```
argv);
      return RUN_ALL_TESTS();
}


/**********
Basic binary search function. This will be
used later in the unit tests. The algorithm
will return the first value it finds in the
array.
**********/


int BinarySearch(int ordered_Items[],
unsigned int array_Size, int value)


{
      if(array_Size <= 0 || ordered_Items ==
NULL)
      {
            return KEY_NOT_FOUND;
      }
      //set the low high and mid boundaries
for the array
      int low_boundary = 0;
      int high_boundary = array_Size - 1;
      int mid_boundary = high_boundary / 2;

      //while we didn't find the value in
the array
      while(low_boundary <= high_boundary &&
ordered_Items[mid_boundary] != value)
      {
            //value must be to the right of
      mid
            if(ordered_Items[mid_boundary] <
      value)
            {
                  low_boundary = mid_boundary
            + 1;
            }
```

```
        else
        {
            //value must be to the left
        of mid
            high_boundary =
        mid_boundary - 1;
        }
        //update mid_boundary based on
        if the value is to the right or
        left of our current position
        mid_boundary = (low_boundary +
        high_boundary) / 2;
    }
    //we didn't find the value in the
    array, so return -1
    if(low_boundary > high_boundary)
    {
        mid_boundary = KEY_NOT_FOUND;
    }
    //otherwise we found the value, so
    return the index at which we found it
    return mid_boundary;
}
```

```
/**********
Below are the unit tests. When making a unit
test, I have to use the TEST function to set
it up so the program knows it's a unit test.
With each function I wanted to say what the
function is and what index it should return.
I think it's important to have good names on
unit tests because I should be able to read
the test name without looking at the code in
the function.
**********/
```

```
/**********
Test for finding value in array
**********/
```

```
TEST(BinarySearch,Finding_Value_Ten_In_Array
_Should_Return_Index_One)
{
        EXPECT_EQ(1,BinarySearch(regular_array
,10,4));
}

/**********
Test for finding value not in array
**********/

TEST(BinarySearch,Finding_Value_Not_In_Array
_Should_Return_Negative_One)
{
        EXPECT_EQ(-
1,BinarySearch(regular_array,11,4));
}

/**********
Number at front of list
**********/

TEST(BinarySearch,Finding_Value_in_Front_of_
Array_Should_Return_Zero)
{
        EXPECT_EQ(0,BinarySearch(regular_array
,5,4));
}

/**********
Test for finding value in empty array
**********/

TEST(BinarySearch,Finding_Value_In_Empty_Arr
ay_Should_Return_Negative_One)
{
        EXPECT_EQ(-
1,BinarySearch(initialized_array,11,5));
}
```

```
/* * * * * * * * *
Test for finding value in odd length array
* * * * * * * * * */

TEST(BinarySearch,Finding_Value_In_Odd_Lengt
h_Array_Should_Return_Index_Two)
{
        EXPECT_EQ(2,BinarySearch(odd_length_ar
ray,7,3));
}

/* * * * * * * * * *
Test for finding value in null array
* * * * * * * * * */

TEST(BinarySearch,Finding_Value_In_Null_Arra
y_Should_Return_Negative_One)
{
        EXPECT_EQ(-
1,BinarySearch(nullArray,7,3));
}

/* * * * * * * * * *
Test for finding value in 0 length array
* * * * * * * * * */

TEST(BinarySearch,Finding_Value_In_Zero_Leng
th_Array_Should_Return_Negative_One)
{
        EXPECT_EQ(-
1,BinarySearch(odd_length_array,0,3));
}

/* * * * * * * * *
Test for finding value with array with
negative values
* * * * * * * * * */
```

```
TEST(BinarySearch,Finding_Value_In_Array_Wit
h_Negative_Values_Should_Return_Negative_One
)
{
    EXPECT_EQ(-
1,BinarySearch(array_with_negative_values,7,
-1));
}
```

Christopher Onorati,
Game Designer and C# Programmer

I first met Christopher Onorati as a bright, cheerful, and energetic young college sophomore, already a terrific junior game designer and easily one of the best of my students at working on a cross-discipline team and dealing with the stresses of team projects. Naturally, as soon as I could, I hired him as a Teaching Assistant (TA). Chris proved to be so accomplished at this, he later became a Lead TA, mentoring the more junior TAs and taking on even more responsibilities. After graduating, Chris decided to continue working at our college as Lab Manager while also working as a full-time freelance game designer on a major unannounced game project. I mentioned that he is energetic, right? Working two jobs is not even slightly daunting for this talented young man.

As my fellow faculty and I immediately realized that Lab Manager wasn't enough work for someone as accomplished and efficient as Chris, one of my colleagues found a terrific project for him: writing a toolkit for the Unity engine. This is intended to help freshmen designers work on their very first digital game projects. The toolkit, nicknamed the LPK, has been a fantastic project for Chris. He very kindly rewrote some of the sections for this book to demonstrate that code samples don't all need to be in C++. C# is a perfectly viable language as well, and one that I recommend to junior programmers who are interested in tools work, as C# is commonly used for that purpose.

The following are Chris Onorati's "Aggressive Path Follower" and "Gamepad Rumble" code samples in C#. I love the fact that he wrote with a lot of tooltips in addition to comments, as this code is part of the toolkit for junior designers.

"Aggressive Path Follower" code sample by Christopher Onorati

This is Chris Onorati's "Aggressive Path Follower" code sample in C#. This code sample is intended to help new designers who are working with path following artificial intelligence for the first time on their game projects.

```
/ * * * * * * * * * *
File:
        YPG_AggressivePathFollower.cs
Authors:            Christopher Onorati
Last Updated:       5/5/2019
Last Version:       2018.3.4

Description:

This script causes its owner game object to
follow a predetermined
path of nodes placed by a designer.  This
object will also activate a
very simple hunting AI if a set game object
or tagged game object comes within range.
* * * * * * * * * * /

using UnityEngine;

namespace YPG
{

/**
* CLASS NAME  : YPG_AgressivePathFollower
* DESCRIPTION : Simplistic AI that follows a
predetermined path and can react to
specified game objects or tagged game
objects.
**/
```

```
[RequireComponent(typeof(Transform))]
public class YPG_AggressivePathFollower :
MonoBehaviour
{
/*********************/
    public enum YPG_PathFollowerMoveMode
    {
        SINGLE,
        LOOP,
        LOOP_TELEPORT,
        LOOP_BACKTRACK,
    };
/*********************/

    [Tooltip("Flag to set if the path
follower starts active.")]
    public bool m_IsActive = true;

    [Tooltip("How the path follower will
react once hitting the end of its path.")]
    public YPG_PathFollowerMoveMode
m_MoveMode;

    [System.Serializable]
    public class AggressionProperties
    {
        [Tooltip("Game objects to hunt or
flee from if set.")]
        public Transform[] m_Enemies;

        [Tooltip("Tagged game objects to
hunt or flee from if set.")]
        public string[] m_EnemyTags;

        [Tooltip("Distance at which the path
follower will enter its aggressive state.")]
        public float m_AggressionRange =
10.0f;
```

```
        [Tooltip("Speed (units per second)
for the path follower to move while in an
aggressive state.")]
        public float m_AggressionSpeed =
10.0f;

        [Tooltip("Run from the game
object(s) instead of running towards the
game object(s).")]
        public bool m_IsCoward;

        [Tooltip("Once an enemy game object
is found, do not forget about it.")]
        public bool m_DontForget;
    }

    public AggressionProperties
m_AggressionProperties;

    [Tooltip("Speed of the path follower
when not in a hunting state.")]
    public float m_Speed = 7.0f;

    [Tooltip("Nodes for the path follower to
move between.")]
    public Transform[] m_Nodes;

/********************/

    //Keep track of which object to move
towards.
    int m_iNodeCounter = 0;

    //Flag to detect when the path follower
has reached a node.
    bool m_bReachedNode = false;

    //Flag used for going backwards
detection.
    bool m_bGoingBackwards = false;
```

```csharp
    //Position of the current enemy.
    Transform m_pCurrentEnemyPosition;

/********************/

    //Cached transform component.
    Transform m_cTransform;

    /**
    * FUNCTION NAME: Start
    * DESCRIPTION  : Cache the transform
component.
    * INPUTS       : None
    * OUTPUTS      : None
    **/
    void Start()
    {
        m_cTransform =
GetComponent<Transform>();
    }

    /**
    * FUNCTION NAME: Activate
    * DESCRIPTION  : Activate the path
follower.  Called externally.
    * INPUTS       : None
    * OUTPUTS      : None
    **/
    public void Activate()
    {
        m_IsActive = true;
        Debug.Log("Path follower " +
gameObject.name + " is active.");
    }

    /**
    * FUNCTION NAME: Deactivate
    * DESCRIPTION  : Deactivate the path
follower.  Called externally.
    * INPUTS       : None
```

```
    * OUTPUTS        : None
    **/
    public void Deactivate()
    {
        m_IsActive = false;
        Debug.Log("Path follower " +
gameObject.name + " is deactive.");
    }


    /**
    * FUNCTION NAME: ToggleActiveState
    * DESCRIPTION  : Toggle the active state
of the path follower.  Called externally.
    * INPUTS       : None
    * OUTPUTS      : None
    **/
    public void ToggleActiveState()
    {
        if(m_IsActive)
            Deactivate();
        else
            Activate();
    }


    /**
    * FUNCTION NAME: FixedUpdate
    * DESCRIPTION  : Manages game object
movement.
    * INPUTS       : None
    * OUTPUTS      : None
    **/
    void FixedUpdate()
    {
        //Easy out for if the path follower
is deactive.
        if (!m_IsActive)
            return;

        bool m_bEnemyInRange = false;
```

```
        //Try to avoid trying to detect
enemies in range as much as possible...it is
a bit on the expensive side.
        if(m_pCurrentEnemyPosition &&
Vector3.Distance(m_cTransform.position,
m_pCurrentEnemyPosition.position) <=
m_AggressionProperties.m_AggressionRange)
            m_bEnemyInRange = true;
        else
            m_bEnemyInRange = Notice();

        //Enemy game object found -
attack!...or flee!
        if ((m_pCurrentEnemyPosition &&
m_AggressionProperties.m_DontForget) ||
m_bEnemyInRange)
            Hunt();
        else
        {
            if (m_pCurrentEnemyPosition !=
null)
                m_pCurrentEnemyPosition =
null;

            Move();
            DetectReachNode();
        }
    }

    /**
    * FUNCTION NAME: Move
    * DESCRIPTION  : Manages path follower
movement as it makes its way to the next
node.
    * INPUTS       : None
    * OUTPUTS      : None
    **/
    void Move()
    {
```

```
        //Easy out for when the path
follower has reached a node.
        if (m_bReachedNode)
            return;

        //Easy out for there being no nodes
to move towards.
        if (m_Nodes.Length <= 0)
        {
            Debug.LogWarning("No nodes were
set for the path follower " +
gameObject.name + ".");
            return;
        }

        m_cTransform.position =
Vector3.MoveTowards(m_cTransform.position,
m_Nodes[m_iNodeCounter].position,
Time.deltaTime * m_Speed);

        //Reached goal.
        if (m_cTransform.position ==
m_Nodes[m_iNodeCounter].position)
        {
            m_bReachedNode = true;
            Debug.Log("Path follower " +
gameObject.name + " reached node.");
        }
    }

    /**
    * FUNCTION NAME: Notice
    * DESCRIPTION  : Detect if there are any
enemies within range.
    * INPUTS        : None
    * OUTPUTS       : bool - True/false if an
enemy was found.
    **/
    bool Notice()
```

```csharp
    {
        //Hunt specific game objects.
        for (int i = 0; i <
m_AggressionProperties.m_Enemies.Length;
i++)
        {
            if
(m_AggressionProperties.m_Enemies[i] != null
                && 
Vector3.Distance(m_cTransform.position,
m_AggressionProperties.m_Enemies[i].position
) <=
m_AggressionProperties.m_AggressionRange)
            {
                m_pCurrentEnemyPosition =
m_AggressionProperties.m_Enemies[i];
                return true;
            }
        }

        //Hunt enemy by tag.
        for(int i = 0; i <
m_AggressionProperties.m_EnemyTags.Length;
i++)
        {
        //Ensure the tag is valid.

if(!string.IsNullOrEmpty(m_AggressionPropert
ies.m_EnemyTags[i]))
            {
                GameObject[] taggedObjects =
GameObject.FindGameObjectsWithTag(m_Aggressi
onProperties.m_EnemyTags[i]);

                for(int j = 0; j <
taggedObjects.Length; j++)
                {
                    //Check distance between
all objects of that tag.
```

```csharp
if(Vector3.Distance(m_cTransform.position,
taggedObjects[j].transform.position) <=
m_AggressionProperties.m_AggressionRange)
                        {

m_pCurrentEnemyPosition =
taggedObjects[j].transform;
                            return true;
                        }
                    }
                }
            }

        //No enemies found this frame.
        return false;
    }


    /**
    * FUNCTION NAME: Hunt
    * DESCRIPTION  : Moves the path follower
based on the current enemy position.
    * INPUTS       : None
    * OUTPUTS      : None
    **/
    void Hunt()
    {

if(!m_AggressionProperties.m_IsCoward)
            m_cTransform.position =
Vector3.MoveTowards(m_cTransform.position,
m_pCurrentEnemyPosition.position,
Time.deltaTime *
m_AggressionProperties.m_AgressionSpeed);
        else
            m_cTransform.position =
Vector3.MoveTowards(m_cTransform.position,
m_pCurrentEnemyPosition.position,
Time.deltaTime * -
```

```
m_AggressionProperties.m_AgressionSpeed);
    }

    /**
    * FUNCTION NAME: DetectReachNode
    * DESCRIPTION  : Manages path follower's
next action when reaching a node.
    * INPUTS       : None
    * OUTPUTS      : None
    **/
    void DetectReachNode()
    {
        if (!m_bReachedNode)
            return;

        if (!m_bGoingBackwards)
            m_iNodeCounter++;
        else
            m_iNodeCounter--;

        //Final node has been reached.
Print this information.
        if (m_iNodeCounter > m_Nodes.Length)
            Debug.Log("Path follower " +
gameObject.name + " has reached the end of
its path.");

        //Move back to the first node
manually from the last.
        if (m_iNodeCounter >= m_Nodes.Length
&& m_MoveMode ==
YPG_PathFollowerMoveMode.LOOP)
            m_iNodeCounter = 0;

        //Teleport to the first node in the
sequence and redo movement.
        else if (m_iNodeCounter >=
m_Nodes.Length && m_MoveMode ==
YPG_PathFollowerMoveMode.LOOP_TELEPORT)
```

```
        {
            m_iNodeCounter = 1;
            m_cTransform.position =
m_Nodes[0].transform.position;
        }

        //Go backwards down the path to the
first node.
        else if ((m_iNodeCounter >=
m_Nodes.Length && m_MoveMode ==
YPG_PathFollowerMoveMode.LOOP_BACKTRACK) ||
                (m_iNodeCounter < 0 &&
m_bGoingBackwards))
        {
            if (!m_bGoingBackwards)
                m_iNodeCounter =
m_Nodes.Length - 2;
            else
            {
                Debug.Log("Path follower " +
gameObject.name + " has reached the end of
its path via backwards movement.");
                m_iNodeCounter = 1;
            }

            m_bGoingBackwards =
!m_bGoingBackwards;
        }

        //Still within valid movement range.
Reset flag.
        if (m_iNodeCounter < m_Nodes.Length)
            m_bReachedNode = false;
    }
  }
}
```

"Gamepad Rumble" code sample by Christopher Onorati

This "Gamepad Rumble" code sample is also in C#. I love the fact that he wrote with a lot of tooltips in addition to comments, as this code is part of the toolkit for junior designers.

```
/***********
File:          YPG_GamepadRumble.cs
Authors:       Christopher Onorati
Last Updated:  5/5/19
Last Version:  2018.3.4

Description:
  This script is used to manage gamepad
rumble.  Call
  "Activate" on external scripts to cause
this script
  to begin its effects.
***********/

using System.Collections;
using System.Collections.Generic;
using UnityEngine;
using XInputDotNetPure; /* Access to
gamepads to rumble.*/

namespace YPG
{

/**
* CLASS NAME  : GamepadRumbleStatus
* DESCRIPTION : Stores the current rumble
status for all gamepads.
**/
```

```csharp
public class GamepadRumbleStatus
{

/********************/

    public readonly PlayerIndex m_iID;

    /**
    * FUNCTION NAME: Constructor
    * DESCRIPTION   : Sets ID of the gamepad.
    * INPUTS        : None
    * OUTPUTS       : None
    **/
    public GamepadRumbleStatus(PlayerIndex _ID)
    {
        m_iID = _ID;
    }


    /**
    * FUNCTION NAME: Rumble
    * DESCRIPTION   : Rumble the controller
this class is in charge of tracking.
    * INPUTS        : intensity       -
Intensity of rumble.
    *                      intensityMods -
Modifiers to the intensity of the shake.
    * OUTPUTS       : None
    **/
    public void Rumble(float _intensity,
Vector2 _intensityMods)
    {
        GamePad.SetVibration(m_iID,
_intensity * _intensityMods.x, _intensity *
_intensityMods.y);
    }
}

/**
```

```
* CLASS NAME  : YPG_GamepadRumble
* DESCRIPTION : Script that manages rumble
cycles on gamepads.  A gamepad can support
multiple of these managers.
**/
public class YPG_GamepadRumble :
MonoBehaviour
{

/********************/

    public enum YPG_GamepadNumber
    {
        ONE,
        TWO,
        THREE,
        FOUR,
        ALL,
    }

    public enum YPG_RumbleMode
    {
        CONSTANT,
        FADE_IN,
        FADE_OUT,
    }

    /********************/

    [Header("GamePad Properties")]

    [Tooltip("Which gamepad to rumble?")]
    public YPG_GamepadNumber
m_GamepadsToRumble = YPG_GamepadNumber.ALL;

    [Header("Rumble Settings")]

    [Tooltip("Mode used to rumble the
gamepads.")]
```

```
    public YPG_RumbleMode m_RumbleMode =
YPG_RumbleMode.CONSTANT;

    [Tooltip("Cause rumble to activate when
the start function on this script is
called.")]
    public bool m_ActivateOnStart = false;

    [Tooltip("Only allow this component to
rumble the gamepads selected once.")]
    public bool m_OnlyRumbleOnce = false;

    [Header("Rumble Properties")]

    [Tooltip("Intensity of the shake.")]
    [Range(0.0f, 1.0f)]
    public float m_Intenstiy = 1.0f;

    [Tooltip("Left and right rumble
strengths.")]
    public Vector2 m_RumbleStrengths = new
Vector2(1.0f, 1.0f);

    [Tooltip("How long to vibrate the
gamepad.")]
    public float m_Duration = 1.5f;

    [Tooltip("Cool down duration between
rumble cycles.")]
    public float m_CoolDownDuration = 0.5f;


/*******************/


    //List of gamepads that can rumble.
    List<GamepadRumbleStatus> m_Gamepads =
new List<GamepadRumbleStatus>();

    //Activate flag to check if controllers
are rumbling.
```

```
    bool m_bIsActive = false;

    //Current intensity of the rumble in the
cycle.
    float m_flCurrentCycleIntensity;

    //Keep track of how long the manager has
been rumbling game pads in its current
cycle.
    float m_flCurrentCycleDuration = 0.0f;

    //Flag to check if this component has
ever rumbled game pads.
    bool m_bHasRumbledOnce = false;

    //Flag to check if the script is on cool
down.
    bool m_bIsOnCoolDown = false;

    /**
    * FUNCTION NAME: Start
    * DESCRIPTION   : Sets list of gamepads
to rumble.
    * INPUTS        : None
    * OUTPUTS       : None
    **/
    void Start()
    {
        //Set game pad list.
        if (m_GamepadsToRumble ==
YPG_GamepadNumber.ONE)
            m_Gamepads.Add(new
GamepadRumbleStatus(PlayerIndex.One));
        else if (m_GamepadsToRumble ==
YPG_GamepadNumber.TWO)
            m_Gamepads.Add(new
GamepadRumbleStatus(PlayerIndex.Two));
        else if (m_GamepadsToRumble ==
YPG_GamepadNumber.THREE)
```

```
            m_Gamepads.Add(new
GamepadRumbleStatus(PlayerIndex.Three));
        else if (m_GamepadsToRumble ==
YPG_GamepadNumber.FOUR)
            m_Gamepads.Add(new
GamepadRumbleStatus(PlayerIndex.Four));
        else
        {
            m_Gamepads.Add(new
GamepadRumbleStatus(PlayerIndex.One));
            m_Gamepads.Add(new
GamepadRumbleStatus(PlayerIndex.Two));
            m_Gamepads.Add(new
GamepadRumbleStatus(PlayerIndex.Three));
            m_Gamepads.Add(new
GamepadRumbleStatus(PlayerIndex.Four));
        }

        //Activate on start
        if(m_ActivateOnStart)
            Activate();
    }

    /**
     * FUNCTION NAME: Update
     * DESCRIPTION  : Manages active cycle
rumbling.
     * INPUTS       : None
     * OUTPUTS      : None
     **/
    void Update()
    {
        //Cycle ending.
        if(m_bIsActive &&
m_flCurrentCycleDuration > m_Duration)
        {
            Deactivate();
            m_bIsOnCoolDown = true;
            StartCoroutine(CoolDown());
```

```
        }

        //Continue active cycle.
        else if(m_bIsActive)
        {
            m_flCurrentCycleDuration +=
Time.deltaTime;
            RumbleGamePads();
        }
    }


    IEnumerator CoolDown()
    {
        yield return new
WaitForSeconds(m_CoolDownDuration);
        m_bIsOnCoolDown = false;
    }


    /**
     * FUNCTION NAME: RumbleGamePads
     * DESCRIPTION  : Rumbles gamepads based
on the state of the current cycle.
     * INPUTS       : None
     * OUTPUTS      : None
    **/
    void RumbleGamePads()
    {
        if (m_RumbleMode ==
YPG_RumbleMode.FADE_IN)
            m_flCurrentCycleIntensity =
(m_flCurrentCycleDuration / m_Duration) *
m_Intenstiy;
        else if (m_RumbleMode ==
YPG_RumbleMode.FADE_OUT)
            m_flCurrentCycleIntensity =
((m_Duration - m_flCurrentCycleDuration) /
m_Duration) * m_Intenstiy;
        else if (m_RumbleMode ==
YPG_RumbleMode.CONSTANT)
```

```
            m_flCurrentCycleIntensity =
m_Intenstiy;

        //Rumble controllers this script has
power over.
        for (int i = 0; i <
m_Gamepads.Count; i++)
        {
            if ((int)m_Gamepads[i].m_iID !=
(int)m_GamepadsToRumble &&
m_GamepadsToRumble != YPG_GamepadNumber.ALL)
                continue;


m_Gamepads[i].Rumble(m_flCurrentCycleIntensi
ty, m_RumbleStrengths);
        }
    }

    /**
     * FUNCTION NAME: Activate
     * DESCRIPTION   : Called by an external
script to start a rumble cycle.
     * INPUTS        : None
     * OUTPUTS       : None
     **/
    public void Activate()
    {
        //Easy out for only rumble once
setting.
        if(m_OnlyRumbleOnce &&
m_bHasRumbledOnce)
        {
            Debug.Log("Script has been set
to only rumble once, and script has already
caused a rumble cycle.");
            return;
        }
```

```
        //Easy out for cool down.
        if(m_bIsOnCoolDown)
        {
            Debug.Log("Script is on cool
down.  Activation request ignored.");
            return;
        }

        m_bIsActive = true;
        m_bHasRumbledOnce = true;
        m_flCurrentCycleDuration = 0.0f;

        //Set initial intensity based on
rumble mode.
        if (m_RumbleMode ==
YPG_RumbleMode.CONSTANT || m_RumbleMode ==
YPG_RumbleMode.FADE_OUT)
            m_flCurrentCycleIntensity =
m_Intenstiy;
        else
            m_flCurrentCycleIntensity =
0.0f;

        Debug.Log("Starting gamepad
rumble.");
    }

    /**
     * FUNCTION NAME: Deactivate
     * DESCRIPTION  : Stop gamepads this
script had power over from rumbling.
     * INPUTS       : None
     * OUTPUTS      : None
     **/
    public void Deactivate()
    {
        m_bIsActive = false;

        for (int i = 0; i <
```

```
m_Gamepads.Count; i++)
        {
            if ((int)m_Gamepads[i].m_iID !=
(int)m_GamepadsToRumble &&
m_GamepadsToRumble != YPG_GamepadNumber.ALL)
                continue;

            m_Gamepads[i].Rumble(0.0f, new
Vector2(0.0f, 0.0f));
        }

        Debug.Log("Stopping gamepad
rumble.");
    }

    /**
    * FUNCTION NAME: OnApplicationQuit
    * DESCRIPTION  : Stop game pad rumble
when the game is exited.
    * INPUTS       : None
    * OUTPUTS      : None
    **/
    void OnApplicationQuit()
    {
        Deactivate();
    }

    /**
    * FUNCTION NAME: OnDestroy
    * DESCRIPTION  : Stop any rumble that
may be happening if the object this
component is on gets destroyed.
    * INPUTS       : None
    * OUTPUTS      : None
    **/
    void OnDestroy()
    {
        if(m_bIsActive)
        {
```

```
            Deactivate();
            Debug.Log("Turning off active
rumbles as the manager component has been
destroyed.");
        }
      }
    }

}    //YPG
```

PART FOUR

Beyond the Basics of Code Samples

I believe that code samples are a great addition to your job-hunting portfolio, but you should not stop there. Let's explore some other possibilities...

GitHub and Other Public-Facing Code Repositories

If you have a relatively compact personal software project that is a tool or otherwise something that might be of use to other programmers, you might want to consider creating a code repository and making your code available as open source.

There are definitely some advantages to this. You'll be able to show off your complete architecture, and also all of the supporting materials that you should have with a complete project... documentation, test cases, and possibly the research you did prior to starting the project.

A tool project will also be a chance for you to demonstrate your ability to work with user interfaces and create a positive user experience. There's a lot to be said for proving that you have these skills and that your focus is on the end-user of your tools.

This is also potentially a way for you to get a lot of feedback on your code!

There are disadvantages, however. With a larger project than the small code samples I've discussed earlier, your code may not be as much of a polished and gorgeous little gem of programming excellence. But prospective employers will get a better idea of what your code will look like when you start working on their software projects.

Working on Larger Open Source Projects

Another great option is to contribute to a larger open source project. There are some really incredible projects out there, and you are likely find one you'll be really passionate about. Another major plus is that you'll be working with other programmers, demonstrating your abilities to work on a large and potentially very complex project, and receive direct feedback on your work from the other programmers on the project.

This is all great! My only concern is that you make sure you track your individual contribution so you can clearly demonstrate what you personally wrote. You may want to consider writing an article or developer blog posts on your experience with a large open source project, so you can talk in detail about your specific work and what you learned while working on the project.

Code Tests from a Prospective Employer

Some companies (Google and Amazon, as of this writing) may ask you to do a code test, where you solve a problem online in a limited timeframe. You'll have to decide whether you think that's something you're willing to do. In general, I recommend agreeing to do a code test as a good investment of your time, even if you don't get an interview. You will likely learn something while working on the test that may help you when talking to the next prospective employer.

But the main reason I bring up this topic is that the completed code test probably should NOT be part of your portfolio! Be careful to maintain the employer's confidentiality, and also check whether it's okay for you to have someone review your code test before submitting it. Basically, respect the process that the employer has set up for this kind of interview.

Code Samples as a Starting Point

Whether you decide to publish an open source project or contribute to a larger open source project, I recommend starting with a code sample first. This will be a smaller effort that you can likely finish and have ready earlier for review and feedback, something that you can polish into that lovely gem of technical excellence. Then, perhaps, you should consider starting a larger complete personal project or contributing to a big open source project.

A Truly Terrible Code Sample: "HeckBuzz"

Before I wrap up this book, I wanted to share with you one of the most wonderfully awful things I've ever seen. My friend Cal Reinhard offered to write the world's worst code sample for this book. Cal is a fantastic programmer at PopCap Games, and this code sample is NOT representative of Cal's excellent programming skills!

"HeckBuzz" is Cal's hilariously bad implementation of a solution for the rather infamous "FizzBuzz" problem. "FizzBuzz" is actually a fairly common question that will come up in a whiteboard programming interview... it's quick and easy, but is sufficient to show a junior programmer's ability to write code and demonstrate their other good qualities as a potential hire. Larger companies like Microsoft will have their own programming problems for their candidates, but my DigiPen students have been asked to program variations of "FizzBuzz" in actual job interviews.

The "FizzBuzz" problem is very straightforward: Print the numbers from 1 to 15. For every multiple of 3, print "Fizz" instead. For every multiple of 5, print "Buzz" instead. If the number is a multiple of 3 and 5, then print "FizzBuzz".

The output from "FizzBuzz" is very simple and obvious. Just print the output on the following page:

```
1
2
Fizz
4
Buzz
Fizz
7
8
Fizz
Buzz
11
Fizz
13
14
FizzBuzz
```

For this implementation, to improve readability, Cal printed each output item on a separate line, as adding formatting is always a nice touch.

So here we go into the depths of awfulness with "HeckBuzz"...

"HeckBuzz" by Cal Reinhard

```cpp
// The "worst" FizzBuzz
#include <iostream>

void FizzBuz(int number) {
    bool didThing = false;
    if (number % 3 == 0) {
        std::cout << "Fizz";
        didThing = true;
    }

    if(number % 5 == 0)
    {
        std::cout << "Buzz";
        didThing = true;
    }

    // We didn't do the thing
    if (!didThing) {
        std::cout << number << std::endl;
    }
    else
       std::cout << "\n";
}

int main()
{
    for (int i = 1; i < 16; ++i) //test
        {
        FizzBuz(i);
        }
}
```

Okay, let's review all the ways in which Cal's code sample is a truly bad solution:

- FizzBuz: The function name is a typo of the name of the problem, "FizzBuzz".

- didThing: It's at least human readable, so it has that going for it. But it is not descriptive. The "thing" in this case is checking whether it's true or false if the integer is evenly divisible by 3 or 5. I'm confident you can come up with a better name than "thing"! (And really, you should!)

- How do you end a line? `std::endl;` is acceptable. `std::cout << "\n";` is acceptable. Using BOTH is bad practice.

- // We didn't do the thing: Commenting your code is good. Incomprehensible comments, though, are not such a good idea.

- //test: Whaaaat? What are we trying to say with this comment? Is it a reminder to test the code manually? Or just some intriguing randomness thrown into the code?

- Braces: Braces everywhere! Cal used a variety of coding styles, intended to make any hiring manager just grit their teeth in pain. My recommendation is to always just pick one style and stay with it.

- int number: "Number" is a very vague way of naming your integer. Better to be specific.

"HeckBuzz" really is exceptional as a "makes your teeth hurt" kind of bad short code sample. Though if you want to see a substantially more extensive example of a terrible code sample, I recommend searching online for "FizzBuzz Enterprise Edition." It is truly a masterpiece of its literary genre.

But in any case, I tip my hat to my friend Cal for this lovely and horrifying code sample!

In Conclusion

If you take nothing else from this book... please, please, PLEASE follow my earnest recommendation that you should always **ask for help** when working on your code samples!

I've talked about how everyone working on code samples will need to ask for help. You need friends and colleagues to review your code samples for you. I know that asking for help isn't always easy. But if your options are losing the great job opportunity in front of you, versus getting up your courage to ask for help from someone whose opinion you value, you know which I'll recommend. Consider this book as an example and trust me; I've asked for a lot of help on this project!

So please, ask for help. Ask for lots of help. Then ask for even more help! If you think you're asking for too much help, you're probably doing it right.

Also, if this book has been useful to you, please pay it forward in some way. Help another junior programmer with their code samples and in their job hunt. You'll be doing a good deed, but I can also guarantee you'll learn something new about programming and code samples in the process. Explaining something to someone is the best way to make sure you really understand it. That's actually how I got into teaching in the first place. I would call up my friend at DigiPen Institute of Technology, Professor Jen Sward, and tell her that I was trying to learn something new like mobile game monetization best practices, and could I come talk to her students about it? The process of making sure I understood the topic well enough to explain it to others would always guarantee that I thoroughly understood it, too.

"Ask for Help" and "Offer Help" are a big deal at my college. My co-teachers and I give out bonus points for doing those in our projects class, as "software engineering and design best practices." So again, don't hesitate to ask for help. And when you can, please help others as well.

If this book was of value to you, please give it an online review. This will help raise the visibility of this book to other new professional programmers who might benefit from it.

Now go out there and write some great code samples!

-Ellen Guon Beeman
Redmond, Washington

About the Author

Ellen Guon Beeman teaches game software design and production as a Senior Lecturer at DigiPen Institute of Technology in Redmond, Washington. She is an expert and consultant in game software development and has worked on 50+ shipped games.

She joined Origin to write and direct games in the Wing Commander series, and has also held salaried positions at Electronics Arts, Warner Bros., Microsoft, Gazillion, and Glu Mobile. As a freelance game designer, she worked on projects for Disney, Sega, Leapfrog Toys, and other companies. Prior to her games career, Ellen was a television writer, and she also has published four fantasy and science fiction novels and numerous short stories. Ellen has been a frequent speaker at the Game Developer Conference, PAX and PAX Dev, and other game industry events.

www.ingramcontent.com/pod-product-compliance
Lightning Source LLC
Chambersburg PA
CBHW031212160726
47992CB00006B/2705